Anchors for PTSD

Building a Life of Safety, Stability, and Strength

Dr. Cindy H. Carr, D.Min. MACL

The Anchored Series

This book is published by **CHC Connect**.

Printed in the United States of America
First Edition, 2026

ISBN: 978-1-971192-32-1

For permissions or inquiries, contact:
Cindy H. Carr
cindyhcarr@outlook.com
www.cindyhcarr.com

About the Anchors Series

The Anchors series exists to help people live steady in the face of mental illness through practical tools, clear language, and compassionate support.

Each diagnosis-specific volume offers a structured set of Anchors (principles + practices) tailored to a particular struggle.

- *Anchors for Bipolar Disorder*
- *Anchors for Major Depressive Disorder*
- *Anchors for PTSD*
- *Anchors for Anxiety*
- *Anchors for ADHD*

Anchors of Support is written for the people who walk alongside someone living with mental illness—family, friends, ministry leaders, and helpers.

Anchors of Faith is the spiritual companion across the whole series. It is designed for readers who want to walk with God day-to-day while also taking mental health seriously as a real clinical reality.

Dedication

To everyone living with PTSD, especially those who wake up braced for danger and still keep showing up, this book is for you.

And to the loved ones who stay close, learn the language of triggers and support, and offer steady presence with clear boundaries, thank you for being part of the healing journey.

May these Anchors help you find safe enough moments, rebuild trust in your body and in others, and return to your life with strength, dignity, and hope.

Table of Contents

How to Use This Book

This book uses twelve named Anchors. They are not steps you complete in order. PTSD recovery is rarely linear. Most people cycle: grounding, then connection, then a small approach step, then back to body basics, then meaning, then maintenance. The skill is returning. Each Anchor chapter follows a consistent rhythm so you can trust the structure even when you do not feel steady:

- A clear Anchor statement (the steady truth).
- An explanation of what it protects you from and why it matters in PTSD.
- One or two practical skills to practice.
- A simple plan for the week (small and doable).
- A check-in to help you notice growth without perfection.

Go slowly. PTSD heals through small steps repeated over time. Fast intensity is not the goal.

Chapter 1
Connection: The Healing Container

Anchor 1 — Connection
Support is one of the ways PTSD is treated

Needing support does not mean you are 'too broken.' It means your nervous system is responding to real threat learning—and support is one of the ways PTSD is treated.

This anchor protects against isolation, shame spirals, unsafe solo trauma work, and dropping out of recovery when symptoms intensify. Trauma teaches the nervous system that danger is everywhere and trust is risky. Safe connection helps the body regulate, helps the mind stay oriented in the present, and helps practice continue long enough for change to take root.

PTSD is not only about what happened in the past. It is about what the nervous system learned about safety, trust, and survival—and how those lessons often push people into isolation. After trauma, many people pull inward. They stop explaining. They stop asking for help. They tell themselves they should be stronger, quieter, more grateful, or "over it." PTSD thrives in that silence.

This book begins with Connection because healing from PTSD is not meant to be done alone. Connection is not simply comfort or reassurance. It is containment. It is accountability. It is the relational safety that makes the rest of the work—especially anything involving memory, emotion, or meaning—possible.

Connection does not mean you have to tell your story to everyone. It means you are not carrying the work of healing by yourself.

Why Connection Matters in PTSD

PTSD affects relationships in both obvious and subtle ways. Some people withdraw. Others cling tightly out of fear of abandonment. Some avoid talking about what happened. Others replay it repeatedly, searching for relief. Many people oscillate between needing support and feeling like a burden.

This is not a character flaw. These are survival patterns.

Research consistently shows that social support is one of the strongest protective factors in PTSD recovery. At the same time, PTSD symptoms can strain relationships and reduce support over time. This creates a painful loop: the more symptoms increase, the more isolated a person feels—and the more isolated they feel, the harder recovery becomes.

Connection interrupts that loop.

The Trauma Team: Who Helps and How

PTSD recovery works best when support is intentional. Instead of relying on one person to meet every need, think in terms of a small team with clear roles. Not everyone needs every role, and one person may fill more than one—but clarity matters.

Your professional support may include a trauma-informed therapist, psychologist, psychiatrist, or primary care provider. Their role is to guide treatment, help with trauma processing, monitor safety, and adjust care when symptoms change.

Your personal support team may include:

- A primary support person (partner, friend, family member) who offers presence and encouragement.
- An accountability partner who helps you follow through on practice.
- A practical helper for specific tasks during high-symptom periods.
- A spiritual or community support person, if meaningful to you.

Support works best when people know what helps—and what doesn't.

What Helps vs. What Hurts

Helpful support usually includes:
• Calm presence without pressure to "fix".
• Encouragement for skills and therapy follow-through.
• Respect for pacing and boundaries.
• Willingness to sit with discomfort without escalating fear.

Unhelpful support often includes:
• Repeated reassurance ("You're fine, it's over, don't think about it").
• Pressuring someone to talk before they're ready.
• Minimizing or comparing trauma.
• Becoming the sole container for intense emotional processing.

This book is designed to help you clarify these differences so support strengthens recovery rather than unintentionally reinforcing symptoms.

Using This Book Alongside Therapy

If you are working with a therapist, this chapter invites collaboration. You might:
• Share which anchors you're practicing.
• Bring worksheets or reflections to sessions.
• Ask your therapist how to pace at-home work.
• Clarify which practices are appropriate between sessions.

If you are not currently in therapy, this chapter helps you prepare. It can support stabilization, understanding symptoms, and building readiness—but it is not a substitute for trauma-informed care.

A Safety and step-up Plan

Connection includes knowing when to ask for more help.

Consider stepping up professional support if:
- Symptoms are worsening week to week.
- You experience frequent dissociation or loss of time.
- Nightmares, panic, or intrusive memories feel unmanageable.
- You are using substances to cope most days.
- You have thoughts of harming yourself or feel unsafe. (American Psychiatric Association, 2022).

Seeking help early is a strength. PTSD deserves care.

Anchor Exercise: Build Your Support Map

Take a few minutes to write down:
- My primary professional support (name/contact).
- My primary personal support person.
- What helps me most when symptoms spike.
- What I'm asking others not to do.
- How I will ask for help this week.

You may return to this map often. It can change over time.

Anchor Plan: One Connection Practice This Week
- Identify one support person and clarify one helpful role.
- Share one sentence about how they can support you.
- Schedule one brief check-in that is not crisis-driven.

Anchor Check
- I can name at least one person who supports my recovery.
- I know what kind of help is most useful to me.
- I have a plan for stepping up support if needed.
- I practiced one intentional connection this week.

Connection is not weakness. It is how nervous systems heal—together.

Chapter 2
Grounding: Coming Back to the Present

Anchor 2 — Grounding
This is a memory, not a current threat.

This anchor protects against flashback fusion, dissociation spirals, and the sense that you are trapped in the past. In PTSD, the alarm system can misread “reminder” as “repeat.” Grounding restores time and place. It helps you regain choice.

After trauma, the past can feel louder than the present. You may be standing in a normal room, talking to someone you trust, and suddenly your body acts as if you are back there. Or you may feel the opposite: numb, far away, unreal—like you are watching your life through glass. PTSD can pull you into two common states: flooding (too much) or shutting down (too little). Grounding is how you come back.

Grounding is not positive thinking. It is not forcing yourself to “calm down.” It is a practical set of skills that helps your brain and body answer one essential question: “Am I safe right now?” When grounding works, your nervous system begins to update from “danger is happening” to “danger happened.”

This chapter is designed to be used early and often—especially on days when symptoms feel loud. If you do not know what anchor you need today, grounding is a safe place to begin. It also supports the later anchors: body regulation, approach practice, and memory work. If you are working with a trauma-informed therapist, share this chapter and choose one or two grounding skills to practice between sessions.

What Grounding Is (and What It Isn't).

Grounding is the skill of orienting—turning your attention to the present environment and your current body in a way that reduces threat confusion. It has three goals:
1) Reconnect you to "now."
2) Reduce escalation (flooding) or thaw shutdown (numbing).
3) Return you to your next right step (a choice you can take).

Grounding is not avoidance. You are not grounding to erase memories or never feel anything. You are grounding so you can feel things without being overwhelmed and so you can continue life and treatment with steadiness.

Recognize Your State: Flooding vs. Shutdown

Before choosing a grounding tool, it helps to name which direction your nervous system is going. Trauma responses often move along a spectrum.

Flooding (high activation) can look like: racing heart, panic, shaking, hypervigilance, rapid thoughts, feeling trapped, urgent need to escape, intrusive images, intense fear or anger.

Shutdown (low activation) can look like: numbness, fog, heaviness, "I don't care," spacing out, feeling unreal, losing track of time, difficulty speaking, dissociation, going blank.

The grounding tool should match the state. Flooding usually needs downshift and orientation. Shutdown often needs gentle activation and reconnection.

Grounding Skill 1: Orienting to Time and Place

When PTSD pulls you into the past, begin with simple orientation statements. Say them out loud if you can. Your voice is a powerful cue to the nervous system.

Orienting script:
- My name is ________.
- Today is ________.
- I am in ________ (place).
- I am ________ years old.

• The trauma happened then. Right now, I am here.
• I can see ________ (name three objects).
• I can feel my feet on the floor.

You are not trying to convince yourself of safety through logic. You are giving your brain clear sensory and cognitive signals that it can use to re-map the moment.

Grounding Skill 2: The 5–4–3–2–1 Reset

This is a classic grounding practice because it engages the senses and moves attention outward—away from internal threat scanning.

5–4–3–2–1:
• 5 things you can see.
• 4 things you can feel (fabric, chair, feet, hands).
• 3 things you can hear.
• 2 things you can smell.
• 1 thing you can taste (or one slow sip of water).

If your mind tries to rush, slow down on the "feel" category. Touch is often the fastest bridge back to the present.

Grounding Skill 3: Temperature and Pressure

The nervous system responds quickly to temperature and firm, safe pressure. These tools can be especially helpful in high activation.

Try one:
• Hold a cold drink or ice cube wrapped in a paper towel for 30–60 seconds.
• Splash cool water on your face.
• Step outside for fresh air and feel the temperature change.
• Press your palms together firmly for 10 seconds, then release.
• Wrap in a weighted blanket (if it feels safe for you).

If you have a history of panic around bodily sensations, use temperature gently and pair it with orienting statements ("This is my body responding; I am here now.").

Grounding Skill 4: Movement as Orientation

Trauma can trap the body in freeze. Small, deliberate movement can remind the nervous system that the present is different from the past.

Choose one small movement sequence:
• Stand up, feel your feet, and slowly shift weight left and right.
• Walk to a doorway and back, naming what you see.
• Stretch your hands and shoulders, then shake out your arms for 10 seconds.
• If shutdown is present, try a brisk 60–90 second walk and then re-orient to the room.

Movement is not about burning off anxiety. It is about reclaiming agency: “My body can move in the direction I choose.”

Grounding Skill 5: A “Sensory Kit” for the Real World

PTSD rarely waits for a quiet moment. Many people benefit from a small grounding kit they can carry or keep nearby. The purpose is not to avoid life—it is to stay in life.

Ideas:

- A strong mint or gum.
- A textured object (smooth stone, worry coin, fabric square).
- A calming scent (lavender, peppermint) if tolerated.
- A grounding card with your orienting script.
- Headphones with one steady playlist.
- A small bottle of water.

Your kit should be simple and personal. If an item becomes a safety behavior that you cannot function without, talk with your therapist about tapering it over time. Early in recovery, support is okay. Later, we practice flexibility.

When Grounding Needs Extra Support: Dissociation and "Losing Time"

Some people experience dissociation as part of PTSD: feeling unreal, detached from the body, or missing chunks of time. If you frequently lose time, feel unsafe, or have a history of self-harm, grounding skills are still useful—but professional support becomes even more important.

If dissociation is common for you, consider these additions:

- Use your name and age in the orienting script (this strengthens identity continuity).
- Use stronger sensory cues (cold water, textured objects) while staying gentle.
- Ground with another person (a voice, a shared activity) whenever possible.
- Practice grounding daily when you are calm, not only during crisis.

If grounding increases distress, that is not failure. It may mean your system needs a slower pace, different tools, or more containment. Bring that information to your therapist. It is valuable data.

The 90-Second Rule: Let the Wave Peak

Many trauma surges peak and shift faster than they feel in the moment. A simple practice is to give your body 90 seconds to move through the first wave while you stay oriented. You are not waiting for anxiety to disappear. You are waiting for the peak to soften so you can choose your next step.

90-second practice:
• Name it: "This is a surge."
• Orient: "I am here now."
• Breathe normally (no forced deep breathing).
• Use one grounding tool (touch, temperature, movement).
• After 90 seconds, choose one small next step.

Anchor Exercise: Your Flashback / Surge Plan (One Page).

Write a short plan you can follow when the past grabs you. Keep it simple enough to use under stress.

My early signs (what I notice first): ________
My best grounding tool for flooding: ________
My best grounding tool for shutdown: ________
My orienting statement: "__________"
Who I will contact if needed: ________
What I will do after the surge (one next step):

____

Anchor Plan: Grounding Practice This Week

1) Practice grounding once daily for 3 minutes when you are already okay. (This trains the pathway before you need it.)
2) Choose one tool for flooding and one tool for shutdown.
3) Write your orienting script on a note in your phone or on a card.
4) Use the 90-second practice once when a surge hits (then return to your day).

Anchor Check

- I can name the difference between flooding and shutdown.
- I have an orienting script I can use when the past intrudes.
- I practiced one sensory grounding tool this week.
- I created a simple surge plan.
- I used grounding to return to a next right step (not to erase feelings).

Closing reminder: You are not back there. Your body is responding to learned danger. Grounding is how you come home to the present—again and again.

Chapter 3
Safety: Safe Enough, Right Now

Anchor 3 — Safety
Right now, in this moment,
I am safe enough to take my next step.

This anchor protects against panic escalation, unsafe "push through" exposure, re-traumatization, and the belief that you must feel completely calm before you can live your life. PTSD often tries to convince you that safety is all-or-nothing. Recovery teaches the opposite: safety can be partial, practical, and real—enough to choose one next step.

After trauma, "safe" can feel like a word other people use—something meant for someone else. Your mind may know the danger is over, but your body may still scan for threats. You may feel jumpy, watchful, braced for impact, or unable to relax even in places that used to feel familiar. Safety is not a switch you flip. In PTSD, safety is something you rebuild—moment by moment, choice by choice.

Safety work is not about pretending nothing bad happened. It is about teaching your nervous system a new pattern: "Right now, in this moment, I am safe enough to take my next step." Safe enough does not mean perfect. It means your body has enough stability and support to stay in the present and keep moving toward healing.

This chapter is here for the days when you feel exposed—when your alarm system is loud, your environment feels threatening, or your relationships feel shaky. Safety is also a foundation for later work. When safety is strengthened, grounding works better, your body recovers faster, and approach practice becomes possible without overwhelming you.

Safety in PTSD: What We Mean (and What We Don't).

In this book, safety has three layers: (1) physical safety, (2) relational safety, and (3) nervous-system safety. Sometimes the environment is genuinely unsafe. Sometimes the environment is safe but your body is reacting to learned danger. And sometimes both are true at once. Your job is not to argue with your alarm system. Your job is to build enough real safety that your system can begin to trust the present.

Safety is not avoidance disguised as wisdom. Avoidance says, "I will never go near anything that reminds me of danger." Safety says, "I will create the conditions that make healing possible, and I will approach life in paced, supported steps."

Layer 1: Physical Safety (The Non-Negotiables).

Physical safety is the foundation. If you are currently in a situation where you are being harmed—emotionally, physically, sexually, or through threats—your first step is not exposure or memory work. Your first step is safety planning and support. trauma-informed care honors reality. If danger is present, we address danger.

If you ever feel at risk of harming yourself, or you worry you might act on suicidal thoughts, seek urgent help immediately. Reach out to local emergency services, a crisis line, or a trusted professional. Getting rapid support is not failure—it is protection.

Practical physical safety steps may include: changing locks, securing digital accounts, adjusting routines, getting medical care, moving toward supportive housing, or creating a plan to leave an unsafe environment. If you are unsure whether your situation is unsafe, a therapist, advocate, or trusted professional can help you assess and plan.

Questions to Ask a trauma-informed Therapist

- How do you pace trauma work so we stay within my window of tolerance?
- How will we handle dissociation, shutdown, or flooding if it happens in session?

- What should I do between sessions when memories or nightmares increase?
- How will we measure progress and decide when to step up or adjust care?

Layer 2: Relational Safety (Who Gets Access to You).

PTSD can make relationships feel dangerous. Some people withdraw from everyone. Others stay in unsafe relationships because the nervous system mistakes familiarity for safety. Relational safety means making intentional choices about who gets access to your story, your time, and your vulnerable moments.

Relational safety does not require perfect relationships. It requires clarity. Ask yourself: Do I feel respected? Do I feel pressured? Do I feel safer after contact, or more dysregulated? Do I feel believed and supported?

If someone repeatedly minimizes your experience, mocks your symptoms, pressures disclosure, or uses your vulnerability against you, that is not a safe container for healing. It may be appropriate to set boundaries, reduce contact, or seek outside help to navigate the relationship.

Layer 3: Nervous-System Safety (Regulating the Alarm).

Sometimes you are physically safe and relationally safe, and your body still feels unsafe. This is common in PTSD. Your alarm system learned danger through experience. It can fire in response to reminders—sounds, smells, places, anniversaries, facial expressions, bodily sensations—without your permission.

Nervous-system safety is built through: grounding (Chapter 3), body basics (sleep, movement, nourishment), predictable routines, and repeated experiences of "I can be activated and still return." Over time, these experiences re-train your system.

Safe Enough vs. "Perfectly Safe"

Many people with PTSD get trapped in a quest for perfect safety. Perfect safety is not possible in human life. The goal is not to eliminate all risk. The goal is to reduce unnecessary risk and build capacity to tolerate uncertainty without collapse.

A useful question is: "What would safe enough look like for the next 10 minutes?" Safe enough might mean: sitting with your back to a wall, turning on a light, asking someone to stay nearby, putting your feet on the floor, or choosing a calmer route home. Safe enough is small and specific.

Safety Behaviors vs. Safety Supports

In anxiety work, we often talk about "safety behaviors" (checking, reassurance, avoidance) that reduce fear short-term but maintain it long-term. In PTSD, the concept needs nuance. Some strategies are protective and appropriate, especially early. The question is: is this helping me stay in life and move toward healing, or is it shrinking my world over time?

Safety supports (often helpful):
- Grounding tools that help you stay present.
- A planned check-in with a therapist or support person.
- A safe exit plan for a difficult event.
- Boundaries that reduce exposure to harmful people.
- A calm, predictable routine after triggers.

Safety behaviors (often maintaining symptoms):
- Avoiding all reminders indefinitely.
- Compulsive scanning, checking, researching, or reassurance loops.
- Using alcohol/substances to numb regularly.
- Never sleeping, never resting, never letting the body downshift.
- Keeping life so small that you stop encountering evidence of safety.

This is not about shame. Many safety behaviors began as survival. The goal is to keep what protects you and gently taper what traps you.

The window of tolerance: Your Safety Range

Your window of tolerance is the range where you can feel emotion and stay present. PTSD can narrow this window. When you are above the window, you may flood (panic, rage, hypervigilance). When you are below the window, you may shut down (numb, disconnected, collapsed). Safety work expands the window so more life is possible.

A practical rule: if you are consistently flooding or shutting down, reduce intensity. Choose smaller steps. Increase support. Your pace is part of safety.

Anchor Skill: The "Safe Enough" Reset

When you feel unsafe, try this short reset. It combines orienting, choice, and one practical adjustment.

Safe Enough Reset:
1) Name it: "My system is signaling danger."
2) Orient: "I am here now. The danger is not happening right now."
3) Choose one safety support: light, water, seat, wall, exit plan, call/text.
4) Take one next step: breathe normally, ground,

move, or ask for help.
5) Return to the present task when possible.

Repeat as needed. Safety is not a one-time decision. It is a practice of returning.

Anchor Exercise: Your Safety Map (One Page).

Fill this out when you are calm, not only when you are escalated. This becomes your personal "safe enough" plan.

- My early warning signs (what I notice first):
- Places that help me feel safer (where I can go):
- People I can contact (names + numbers):
- Professional supports (therapist/doctor + contact):
- Crisis supports (local emergency / crisis line):
- What helps me most (presence, grounding, walking, quiet):
- What is NOT helpful (what makes it worse):
- Steps to reduce risk (remove/secure harmful items, substances, etc.):
- One sentence to remind myself (hope + next step):

If you already have a safety plan with a clinician, you can copy it here or reference it. The goal is usability: a plan you can follow when thinking is harder.

Anchor Plan: Safety Practice This Week

1) Choose one safety support you will practice daily (lights, grounding, routine, check-in).

2) Identify one trigger situation and create a "safe enough" plan for it (where you'll sit, who you'll text, what you'll do after).
3) Share one piece of your safety map with a trusted support person.
4) If you notice increasing risk (more substances, less sleep, more isolation), step up support early.

Anchor Check

• I can name the difference between real danger and learned danger.
• I know what "safe enough" looks like for me in small moments.
• I created a one-page safety map.
• I practiced one safety support this week.
• I know when and how I will step up support if needed.

Closing reminder: You do not have to earn safety by being perfectly calm. Safe enough is a real place. From safe enough, healing becomes possible.

Chapter 4
Body: Training the Nervous System to Recover

Anchor 4 — Body
My body learned danger. My body can learn recovery.

This anchor protects against chronic hyperarousal, shutdown, exhaustion, and the belief that your body is broken beyond repair. Trauma teaches the nervous system to expect threat. Recovery teaches the system that it can come down, rest, and return to life.

PTSD is not only a story in the mind. It is a pattern in the body. After trauma, many people live with a nervous system that stays on guard—ready to fight, flee, freeze, or shut down. You might feel jumpy, tense, exhausted, restless, numb, or "wired and tired." You may be highly sensitive to sound, touch, crowds, or sudden changes. Even when life is calm, your body may act as if danger is near.

The goal of this chapter is not to make you perfectly relaxed. The goal is to help your body recover more often and more quickly. In PTSD, recovery is the skill: returning from activation into steadiness, again and again. Over time, those returns widen your window of tolerance and make daily life more possible.

This anchor does not replace trauma-focused therapy. It supports it. Body work helps you stay present during treatment, tolerate emotion without flooding or shutting down, and rebuild trust in your own physiology. If you have a therapist, consider choosing one or two body anchors to practice between sessions and track what changes.

The PTSD Body Loop

Many people try to heal PTSD through insight alone: "I know it's over, so why do I still feel this way?" The answer is that the body can hold learning that words do not reach. The PTSD body loop often looks like this:

Trigger or reminder → body alarm (heart, breath, tension, nausea, heat) → threat scanning and urgency → coping response (avoid, numb, control) → temporary relief → increased sensitivity over time.

Body anchors interrupt this loop by creating new learning: "I can feel activation and still return."

Two States to Know: Upshift and Downshift

In the earlier chapters, we named flooding and shutdown. Here we will use two simple terms: upshift and downshift.

Upshift means the nervous system is mobilized: fight/flight energy, agitation, panic, anger, scanning, insomnia, urgency.

Downshift means the nervous system is conserving: numbness, heaviness, fog, disconnection, low energy, collapse, dissociation.

Your goal is not to stay in the middle all the time. The goal is to recognize the state and respond with the right kind of support.

Body Anchor 1: Breath Without Force

Many people with PTSD have complicated relationships with breathing. Some feel panicky when they try to breathe deeply. If that is you, the answer is not "more control." The answer is gentler attention.

Try this:
- Let your breath be natural.
- Place one hand on your chest or abdomen.
- Exhale a little longer than you inhale, without strain.
- Whisper: "I am here now."

Even a small lengthening of the exhale can signal safety to the nervous system. If breath focus increases distress, shift to touch, movement, or sound-based grounding instead.

Body Anchor 2: Sleep as Nervous-System Medicine

Sleep disruption is one of the most common and most punishing PTSD symptoms. Poor sleep increases irritability, startle response, emotional reactivity, and hopelessness. You do not have to have perfect sleep to heal, but consistent sleep support makes every other anchor easier.

Two sleep anchors:

- A wind-down cue (same 10–20 minute routine most nights).
- A wake-time anchor (get up within the same 60–90 minutes daily).

Nightmares are common in PTSD. If nightmares are frequent, tell your clinician. There are evidence-informed therapies and medications that can help, and you deserve support.

Body Anchor 3: Movement That Completes Stress

Trauma can leave the body stuck in unfinished stress responses—freeze that never fully resolves. Gentle, predictable movement can help complete stress and signal to the nervous system that you have agency now.

Choose one:

- A 10-minute walk with orienting (name what you see).

• Stretching your shoulders, neck, and hips for 5 minutes.
• Rhythmic movement (rocking, slow dance, cycling, swimming) if it feels safe.

Movement is not punishment. It is communication to the body: "I can move and return."

Body Anchor 4: Nourishment and Stimulant Boundaries

When the nervous system is activated, appetite may vanish or cravings may increase. Caffeine and stimulants can increase hyperarousal. Alcohol and substances can deepen shutdown and interfere with memory processing and sleep.

This is not a moral issue. It is physiology.

One small practice: choose one supportive boundary this week—such as caffeine only before noon, adding protein at breakfast, or limiting alcohol on nights when sleep is already fragile.

Body Anchor 5: Touch and Safe Pressure

The body often responds to safe pressure and touch—especially when paired with orienting. Some people find relief in a weighted blanket, firm pillow hug, hand-over-heart, or warm shower. Others find touch triggering. Your body gets to decide.

Try one safe option:
- Hand on heart and abdomen.
- Firm self-hug for 10 seconds.
- Warm shower with attention to temperature.
- Weighted blanket for 10 minutes (if soothing).

Touch is not a requirement. It is one possible door back to safety.

Body Anchor 6: The Nervous-System Menu

Many people get stuck trying to find "the one" regulation tool. It is better to build a menu. Different tools work for different states.

Upshift menu (when activated): cool water, longer exhale, grounding, slow walk, dim lights, reduce stimulants, gentle stretching, calming sound.

Downshift menu (when numb/shut down): bright light, cold splash, brief brisk movement, social contact, music with rhythm, purposeful task, warm drink.

Highlight two or three tools that work for you. Put them on a note in your phone. This makes recovery easier when thinking is harder.

When Body Symptoms Need Medical Support

Trauma can live in the body, but not every body symptom is PTSD. If you have chest pain, fainting, severe GI symptoms, sleep apnea symptoms, or new neurological symptoms, seek medical evaluation. PTSD can coexist with medical issues, and you deserve thorough care.

Anchor Exercise: Your Body Recovery Plan (One Page).

Fill this out when you are calm. Keep it short enough to actually use.

- My common upshift signals:
- My common downshift signals:
- My top 3 calming tools:
- My top 3 activating tools:
- My sleep anchor this week:
- One substance or stimulant boundary I'm practicing:
- Who I can contact if I'm not coming down:

Anchor Plan: Body Practice This Week

1) Choose one sleep anchor and practice it 4 nights.
2) Do one 10-minute movement practice on 3 days.
3) Use your menu once during an upshift or downshift.
4) Record one sentence: "When I did ___, my body did ___."

Anchor Check

- I can name my upshift and downshift signals.
- I practiced one sleep support this week.
- I practiced one movement support this week.
- I used at least one tool from my nervous-system menu.
- I recorded one sentence of learning about my body.

Closing reminder: Your body is not betraying you. It is doing its best with what it learned. Recovery is training—not perfection.

Chapter 5
Story: Guilt, Shame, and the Meanings Trauma Leaves Behind

Anchor 5 — Story
Trauma lies in meanings. I can learn to see clearly.

This anchor protects against self-blame spirals, shame-based isolation, and the belief that your symptoms mean you are weak or broken. Trauma often trains people to carry responsibility for what was not their responsibility. This chapter helps you identify those "stuck meanings" and begin loosening them with compassion and clarity.

Trauma is not only what happened. Trauma is also what it made you believe. After a traumatic experience, the nervous system learns danger—but the mind often tries to make sense of danger by creating meanings. Some of those meanings are protective in the short term ("Trust no one," "Stay on guard," "Don't feel anything"). Others become cages ("It was my fault," "I'm ruined," "I should have known," "I deserved it").

In PTSD, the story your brain tells is not always a conscious narrative. It can show up as a feeling of defectiveness, a flash of self-blame, a reflexive apology, or a constant scanning for what you did wrong. Many people carry guilt and shame long after the threat has passed. And if the trauma involved moral conflict, helplessness, or survival when others didn't, the meanings can go even deeper.

This chapter is about separating facts from meanings—so you can keep what is true and release what trauma added. You are not rewriting history. You are updating the interpretation your nervous system and mind attached to the event.

Why Guilt and Shame Are So Common in PTSD

When something terrible happens, the mind often searches for a reason. Blame can feel like control: "If it was my fault, then I can prevent it next time." This is one reason self-blame is so sticky. It can feel safer to believe "I caused it" than to face the truth: something happened that you could not fully control.

Guilt and shame are not the same.

- Guilt says: "I did something wrong."
- Shame says: "I am something wrong."

Guilt can sometimes be useful when it points toward repair. Shame almost never heals anything. Shame drives hiding, disconnection, and hopelessness.

Survivor's Guilt and the Weight of "Why Me?"

Some people with PTSD carry survivor's guilt: "Why did I live?" "Why was I spared?" "I should have done more." This form of guilt is often less about responsibility and more about love, grief, and the unbearable unfairness of loss.

Survivor's guilt often shows up as a mind trying to make meaning out of randomness. It can include a feeling that you don't deserve safety or joy. If you carry this, you are not alone. The goal is not to erase love or grief. The goal is to release the verdict that says you must suffer forever to honor what happened.

When Trauma Becomes Moral Injury

Moral injury is not a formal PTSD diagnosis, but it is a powerful trauma-adjacent experience. It involves the pain of having witnessed, participated in, or been unable to prevent actions that violate your deepest values. For some people, moral injury includes betrayal by leaders or systems that were supposed to protect. (Litz et al., 2009).

Moral injury often carries intense shame, anger, and spiritual struggle. It can feel like, "I am unforgivable," or "The world is morally unsafe." Healing moral injury often involves truth-telling, grief, repair when possible, and meaning-making—not punishment. (Litz et al., 2009).

Stuck Points: The Trauma Rules That Keep You Trapped

A stuck point is a rigid belief that trauma leaves behind. It often sounds absolute. It often begins with always, never, should, or must.

Common stuck points include:
- “It was my fault.”
- “I should have fought harder.”
- “I can’t trust anyone.”
- “I’m permanently damaged.”
- “If I relax, something bad will happen.”
- “My feelings are dangerous.”

These beliefs make sense as survival strategies. They also keep PTSD alive by maintaining threat and avoidance.

The Fact–Meaning Split (A Skill That Changes Everything).

One of the most powerful PTSD skills is learning to separate what happened (facts) from what you concluded about yourself, others, and the world (meanings). Facts are specific and observable. Meanings are interpretations.

Example:
- Fact: “He yelled and blocked the door.”
- Meaning: “I am powerless forever.” The fact may be

true. The meaning may be trauma's exaggeration. Updating meaning does not deny the fact. It prevents the fact from becoming a life sentence.

Try this two-column practice:
Left column: Facts (what a camera would record).
Right column: Meanings (what your mind concluded).

Then ask: Which meanings are protective but outdated? Which meanings are shame-based? Which meanings are absolutely true? Which might be softened?

Responsibility vs. Regret vs. False Guilt

This distinction helps many people with PTSD.

- Responsibility: You had real control and chose harm.
- Regret: You wish something had gone differently.
- False guilt: You feel responsible for what you could not control, for surviving, or for being human under threat.

Many trauma survivors carry false guilt. Trauma often happens in situations with limited choices, coercion, fear, power imbalance, or impossible options. If you did what you could with what you had, that is not moral failure. That is survival.

Reframing Shame: From "What's Wrong With Me?" to "What Happened to Me?"

Shame asks, "What's wrong with me?" trauma-informed healing asks, "What happened to me, and how did my body try to protect me?"

This reframing does not remove responsibility where it belongs. It removes responsibility where it does not belong.

Faith Lens: Condemnation vs. Conviction After Trauma

This book is for people of many faith streams and those with no faith stream. This short section is offered because many trauma survivors experience spiritual accusation.

Condemnation says: "You are ruined. You are disqualified. You deserve pain." It produces hiding, hopelessness, and isolation.

Healthy conviction (when it is real) says: "Something was wrong. Let's move toward truth, repair, and freedom." It produces clarity and hope.

If your inner voice sounds like relentless punishment, that is not the voice of love. Trauma often speaks in accusation. Healing invites a different voice: compassion, truth, and support. If faith is meaningful to you, consider seeking a trusted trauma-informed spiritual leader or counselor who can help you untangle shame from love.

Anchor Exercise:

Use this prompt for one recurring belief.

1) The stuck point:
2) The emotion it brings (0–100):
3) The fact that happened (camera view):
4) The meaning trauma added:
5) Evidence for / evidence against the stuck point:
6) A more balanced truth:
7) One next right step:

Anchor Plan: One Story Update This Week

1) Choose one stuck point you notice often.
2) Use the fact–meaning split once.
3) Write one balanced truth that is compassionate and realistic.
4) Practice one small action that matches the balanced truth (a connection, a boundary, a step outside, a therapy task).

Anchor Check

- I can name one recurring stuck point.
- I can separate facts from meanings.
- I can identify false guilt vs. responsibility.
- I wrote one balanced truth.
- I took one next right step aligned with that truth.

Closing reminder: The trauma happened. The meanings are not all permanent. You can carry truth without carrying a verdict.

Chapter 6
Choice: Reclaiming Agency After Helplessness

Anchor 6 — Choice
I have choices now, even small ones.

This anchor protects against learned helplessness, freeze responses that never release, and the belief that you must wait for symptoms to disappear before living. PTSD often makes life feel reactive. Choice makes life responsive.

Trauma is often defined by the moment choice disappears. Something happens to you, around you, or in front of you—and your nervous system learns a painful lesson: "I am not in control." Even when that belief is understandable, it can become a prison. PTSD can make the world feel like it is run by triggers, symptoms, and sudden body alarms.

This chapter is about reclaiming agency. Not in a dramatic, heroic way. In a small, steady way that teaches the nervous system: "I have choices now." Choice is one of the most powerful antidotes to trauma because it rewires helplessness into capability.

Reclaiming choice does not deny what happened. It honors what happened by refusing to let the trauma remain the only authority in your life.

The Trauma Imprint: Helplessness and Freeze

Many people think of trauma responses as fight or flight. But freeze and submit responses are also common—especially when escape is not possible. The body may go still, numb, compliant, or disconnected. Later, people may blame themselves for that reaction: "Why didn't I fight?"

Freeze is not moral failure. Freeze is nervous-system biology. The brain chooses the response most likely to survive based on the situation, past learning, and available options. Choice work helps you stop judging your survival responses and start building new options for the present.

The Choice Ladder: From Micro-Choice to Life Choice

In PTSD recovery, choice is built like a muscle. You start with micro-choices that are small enough to be possible even when anxious. Over time, these build into larger choices.

Micro-choices (30 seconds to 2 minutes):

- I can plant my feet.
- I can turn my head and look around.

- I can text one person.
- I can take a sip of water.
- I can step outside for fresh air.

Mid-level choices (5 to 20 minutes):
- I can take a short walk.
- I can do a grounding practice.
- I can move my body gently.
- I can return to a task for 10 minutes.
- I can attend part of an event and leave when planned.

Life choices (ongoing):
- I can seek therapy.
- I can reduce contact with unsafe people.
- I can change routines that keep me trapped.
- I can build a life aligned with my values (Chapter 12).

The "Next Right Step" Anchor

Trauma often pushes the mind into extremes: "I must fix everything" or "I can't do anything." The next right step is the antidote. It is the smallest action that moves you toward safety, connection, or growth without overwhelming you.

A next right step might be:
- telling the truth to one safe person,
- taking a planned break instead of dissociating,
- leaving an unsafe conversation,

• returning to one routine after a trigger,
• doing one small exposure step (Chapter 8).

Your next right step is allowed to be small. Small is how we rebuild trust.

Choice vs. Control

PTSD can create a strong desire for control. Control makes sense when you have lived through unpredictability. But control can become exhausting. Choice is different. Choice is flexible. Control says, "Nothing can go wrong." Choice says, "Even if something goes wrong, I can respond."

Recovery is not about controlling every feeling. It is about building confidence that you can respond to feelings without collapsing.

Anchor Skill: The Three Choices Practice

When you feel trapped, try this practice. It helps the brain re-open options.

Three Choices:
1) Name what is happening (facts only): "My body is activated."
2) Name three choices (even tiny): "I can sit, stand, or walk." "I can text, breathe, or drink water."
3) Choose one and do it for 60 seconds.
4) After 60 seconds, reassess: "What is my next right step?"

This is not about perfect choices. It is about breaking the trance of helplessness.

When Choice Feels Unsafe

Some trauma survivors learned that choice led to punishment, danger, or abandonment. If choice itself feels risky, go slower. Start with choices that are private and low-stakes. Practice choice in safe contexts first. If choice triggers intense fear or dissociation, that is important clinical data to bring to therapy.

Anchor Exercise: Your Agency Map (One Page).

Fill this out with honesty. You are not proving strength. You are building a plan.

- Situations where I feel most powerless:
- My common freeze / submit signals:
- Three micro-choices that help me return:
- One mid-level choice I can practice this week:
- One life choice I am considering (with support):
- Who can help me practice choice:

Anchor Plan: One Choice Practice This Week

1) Practice the Three Choices tool once per day for 3 days, even when you are okay.
2) In one trigger moment, choose a next right step instead of collapsing or avoiding completely.
3) Tell one support person what choice you are practicing so they can encourage follow-through.
4) Record one sentence of learning: "When I chose ___, I noticed ___."

Anchor Check

- I can name one place where I feel powerless.
- I identified three micro-choices that help me return.
- I practiced the Three Choices tool at least once.
- I chose one next right step during a trigger moment.
- I recorded one sentence of learning about my agency.

Closing reminder: Trauma took away choice. Recovery returns it. You do not have to wait to feel fearless to begin choosing.

Chapter 7
Approach: Reducing Avoidance and Taking Your Life Back

Anchor 7 — Approach
Avoidance keeps trauma powerful.
Approach gives me my life back.

This anchor protects against world-shrinking, chronic restriction, and the sense that triggers control your choices. Avoidance teaches the brain: "That thing was dangerous; I survived because I escaped." Approach teaches the brain new learning: "I can be near reminders and still be safe enough."

Avoidance is one of the most understandable trauma responses—and one of the most costly. After trauma, your nervous system learns: "Stay away from anything that reminds you of danger." That can include places, people, sensations, emotions, conversations, memories, news stories, smells, anniversaries, or even joy. Avoidance makes sense because it reduces distress in the short term. But over time, avoidance shrinks life.

This chapter is about approach. Approach does not mean forcing yourself into unsafe situations. Approach means turning toward life again in paced, supported steps. It means choosing what matters while your nervous system learns that the present is not the past.

Approach work should be done with wisdom. For many people, especially those with significant dissociation, high risk, complex trauma, or severe symptom spikes, approach practices are safest when planned with a qualified trauma therapist. This chapter is designed to support that work—not replace it.

The Avoidance Loop

Avoidance can look obvious (not driving, not going out, not dating). It can also look subtle: staying busy to avoid feeling, scrolling to numb out, overworking, refusing rest, never being alone, or keeping every conversation shallow.

The loop often looks like this:

Trigger or reminder → body alarm → threat story ("I can't handle this") → avoidance or escape → short-term relief → long-term cost (smaller life, stronger fear).

Approach breaks the loop by creating new experiences of capability.

Approach vs. Flooding: The Window Matters

In PTSD recovery, the goal is not to overwhelm yourself. The goal is to practice within your window of tolerance. If you push too hard and flood, the brain may learn: “That was dangerous.” If you avoid completely, the brain learns: “I can’t handle it.”

Approach is the middle path: small steps that are challenging but doable—repeated until the nervous system updates.

What Counts as Approach?

Approach is any action that moves you toward a valued life while tolerating discomfort. It might include:

- driving one exit further than usual,
- entering a store for two minutes and leaving as planned,
- sitting with your back not to a wall for 30 seconds,
- opening a trauma-related email and reading one paragraph,
- having a five-minute conversation that includes a real feeling,
- noticing a body sensation without immediately trying to stop it.

Approach is not bravery theater. It is training.

Safety Behaviors in PTSD (and How to Taper Gently).

Sometimes people do "approach" while still using strong safety behaviors that prevent new learning—constant checking, scanning exits, repeated reassurance, numbing with substances, or always bringing an escape person who functions as a shield.

In PTSD, we taper with compassion. Some supports are appropriate early. The question is: does this support help you stay in life and learn, or does it become the only way you can function?

A gentle taper principle: reduce one safety behavior by 10–20% during a planned approach step. If you normally check the door lock five times, try four. If you normally stand by the exit the whole time, try two minutes in the middle of the room. If you normally call for reassurance immediately, wait ten minutes first and use grounding.

Building an Approach Ladder

An approach ladder is a list of steps ranked from easier to harder. You start with steps that create mild-to-moderate anxiety and repeat them until they feel more manageable. Then you move up one step.

Use a 0–10 rating for distress. Aim for steps in the 3–7 range. If a step is a 9 or 10, it is likely too much right now. Shrink it until it becomes doable.

Examples (choose what fits your life):

- Level 3: Sit in the car for two minutes and ground.
- Level 4: Drive around the block once.
- Level 5: Enter a store, buy one item, leave.
- Level 6: Attend a small gathering for 15 minutes.
- Level 7: Drive on a highway for one exit.
- Level 8: Sit through a longer meeting without leaving.
- Level 9: Return to a high-trigger location with therapist planning.

How to Run an Approach Practice

Approach works best when it includes clear intention and reflection. Use this simple structure:

1) Name the step: "Today I will ______."
2) Name the prediction: "My anxiety predicts ______."
3) Choose one safety behavior to taper (10–20%).
4) Use grounding as needed—but stay with the step until the planned end.
5) Record learning: "What did I learn about my ability to cope? What happened in reality?"

Learning is the goal, not perfect calm.

When Approach Gets Stuck (and What to Do).

Problem: I'm doing steps but I'm not improving.
Fix: Check safety behaviors. If you are still heavily escaping, checking, or numbing, the brain may not be learning. Reduce one safety behavior slightly.

Problem: I start too hard and burn out.
Fix: Start smaller. Success builds success. Choose a 3–5 step and repeat.

Problem: I use approach to prove I'll never feel triggered again.
Fix: Shift the goal: tolerate discomfort, build coping confidence, and return to life even with symptoms present.

Problem: I feel ashamed that I'm anxious during practice.
Fix: Approach is not a performance. Anxiety is expected. Courage is staying with discomfort while you choose your next step.

Using Support People Without Turning Them Into a Safety Behavior

Support can help approach work, especially early. The healthiest support roles are those that build capability, not dependence.

Healthy roles:

- Coach: helps you plan steps and celebrates effort.

- Buddy: accompanies early steps, then fades support over time.
- Accountability partner: checks in on practice schedule.
- Boundary helper: refuses reassurance loops while offering presence ("I'm here, but I won't answer that again.").

If your support person becomes the only reason you can approach, that's data, not failure. It means we need a gentler ladder and a plan to taper support as you grow.

Anchor Exercise: Your Approach Ladder (One Page).

Create a ladder with at least 10 steps. Use the table below as your template.

Approach Step	Distress (0–10)	Safety Behavior to Taper	Learning (after practice)
1.			
2.			
3.			
4.			
5.			
6.			
7.			
8.			
9.			
10.			

Anchor Plan: Two Approach Practices This Week

1) Build one approach ladder with at least 10 steps.
2) Complete two steps rated 3–7 this week.
3) Reduce one safety behavior by 10–20% during each step.
4) Write one sentence of learning after each practice.
5) Share your practice with one support person or therapist.

Anchor Check

- I can explain why avoidance keeps PTSD strong.
- I built an approach ladder with at least 10 steps.
- I completed at least two approach practices.
- I tapered one safety behavior during practice.
- I recorded learning and chose a next step.

Closing reminder: The goal is not to erase triggers. The goal is to expand your life. Approach is how the nervous system learns freedom.

Chapter 8
Memory: Helping the Brain File the Trauma Correctly

Anchor 8 — Memory
The trauma is over. My brain can learn that.

This anchor protects against flashback fusion, persistent re-living, nightmare cycles, and the belief that if the memory returns, you are failing. In PTSD, the memory often behaves like a present-tense event. Recovery helps the brain update the time-stamp: "then, not now."

PTSD is often described as a disorder of memory and alarm. The danger is over, but the brain and body behave as if it is still happening. You may have intrusive memories, nightmares, flashbacks, or sudden body surges that feel disconnected from the present. You may also experience the opposite—numbness, gaps, or a sense that the event is unreal. All of these can be part of the same problem: the trauma memory has not been fully integrated as "something that happened." (American Psychiatric Association, 2022).

This chapter is a map—not a DIY trauma processing manual. Trauma memory work is powerful, and for many people it is safest and most effective when guided by a qualified trauma-informed clinician. The goal here is to help you understand what "processing" means, what the evidence-based therapies are doing, and how you can support the work at home without accidentally overwhelming your system.

If you are in therapy, this chapter can give you language to collaborate with your clinician. If you are not in therapy yet, it can help you understand why professional support matters and how to build readiness. Either way, you will leave with clear guardrails and a practical plan for supporting your nervous system around memory work.

What Trauma Memories Are Like

Trauma memories often feel different from ordinary memories. Ordinary memories usually have a clear beginning and end. You can remember them and still stay anchored in the present. Trauma memories may arrive in fragments—images, sounds, sensations, or emotions—without context. The body may react as if danger is happening again: heart pounding, breath change, freezing, nausea, shaking, rage, or dissociation.

This does not mean you are weak or broken. It means your brain did what brains do under threat: it prioritized survival over storytelling. The memory was stored in a way that helped you get through the moment. Processing helps you store it differently so it stops hijacking the present.

What "Processing" Really Means

Many people think trauma processing means "talk about it until it stops hurting." That can be misleading. Effective trauma processing is usually structured and paced. It aims to do three things:

1) Reduce avoidance so reminders no longer control your life.
2) Update stuck meanings (guilt, shame, permanent danger).
3) Help the nervous system learn that the trauma is not happening now.

Processing is not about forcing yourself to relive trauma in a raw, uncontained way. It is about building enough stability and support to approach the memory with skill, structure, and compassion.

Evidence-Based Paths: What Therapies Are Doing

Most major clinical guidelines list trauma-focused CBT approaches (including Prolonged Exposure and Cognitive Processing Therapy) and EMDR as first-line treatments for PTSD (Bisson et al., 2019; Department of Veterans Affairs & Department of Defense, 2023; National Institute for Health and Care Excellence, 2018; Schnurr et al., 2024; Shapiro, 2018).

There are several well-supported approaches to PTSD treatment. Different methods use different tools, but they often share common ingredients: safety, pacing, approach, meaning-updating, and repeated "present-time" orientation.

If you hear "Prolonged Exposure (PE)," it is a structured, time-limited therapy that uses imaginal and in-vivo exposure—carefully paced—to help the brain update danger learning and reduce avoidance (Foa et al., 2007).

Some trauma-focused therapies involve approaching trauma memories directly in a controlled way so the brain can update. Others focus on identifying and changing stuck beliefs that keep trauma alive. Some use bilateral stimulation as part of structured processing. The names may differ, but the aim is similar: reduce threat, integrate memory, and restore agency.

If you are unsure what kind of therapy you are receiving, a simple question to ask is: "How does this approach help my brain and body learn the trauma is over?" A good therapist will be able to answer in plain language.

Guardrails: What Not to Do Alone

This is one of the most important sections in the book.

Do not do deep trauma processing alone if any of the following are true:

- You frequently dissociate, lose time, or feel detached from reality.
- You have active self-harm urges or suicidal thoughts.
- You have severe substance use that increases risk.
- Your symptoms escalate into panic or shutdown for long periods.
- You have complex trauma with many events and unclear boundaries.
- You do not have stable support or a safe environment.

In these cases, the safest step is to build Connection (Chapter 2), strengthen Grounding and Safety (Chapters 3–4), and engage a qualified clinician before doing memory-focused work.

Even if you do not meet the criteria above, it is still wise to consult a therapist when possible. This chapter supports you, but it does not replace clinical containment.

The Difference Between Remembering and Re-Traumatizing

A helpful test is the outcome. When trauma work is paced well, you may feel emotional and tired, but you return to steadiness. You have a sense of movement.

When trauma work is uncontained, you may feel flooded, dissociated, ashamed, or unable to function for days. That is not "proof you need to push harder." That is data that the pace or container needs adjustment.

Signs you may need to slow down or increase support:

- You cannot return to the present after practices.
- Sleep collapses for multiple nights.
- You increase substance use to cope.
- Intrusions become more frequent and intense.
- You feel unsafe or hopeless.

How to Support Memory Work at Home (Without Going Too Far).

Many people want something practical they can do at home. Here is what helps most: supporting stability, reducing avoidance in daily life, and strengthening your ability to return to the present.

Four helpful at-home supports:

1) Ground before and after (Chapter 3). If you are going to talk about trauma in therapy, do a short grounding practice beforehand and a longer one afterward. This teaches your system: "We can touch the memory and come back."

2) Use the "container" practice. Before a session, imagine a safe container (box, vault, folder) where you can place trauma material when you are done. After the session, visualize closing the container and returning to the room. This is not denial. It is boundary-setting with the mind.

3) Track your window of tolerance. After sessions or difficult days, rate your level of activation (0–10) and note what helps you come down. This helps you and your therapist calibrate pace.

4) Practice life approach steps (Chapter 8). Memory work works best when it is paired with real-life re-engagement. Even small approach steps help the brain learn: "I am living now."

Nightmares and Sleep After Trauma Work

Nightmares are common in PTSD and can intensify when you begin treatment. If nightmares are severe or worsening, bring it to your clinician. There are therapies and medical options that can help. At home, focus on consistent sleep anchors (Chapter 5) and grounding after waking: lights on, orienting statements, feet on the floor, a sip of water, and a return-to-bed plan.

If you wake in panic, remind yourself: "This is my nervous system replaying a threat. I am here now."

Anchor Skill: The "Then vs. Now" Practice

This practice helps re-time-stamp a memory intrusion without forcing you into it.

Then vs. Now:
1) Name: "This is a trauma memory."
2) Locate: "Where am I right now?" (name the room, date, and your age)
3) Sense: name three present-time sensations (feet, chair, air, sounds)
4) Choose: one next right step (water, text support, step outside, return to task)
5) Close: "The trauma is over. I am safe right now."

Repeat as needed. The repetition is the training.

Anchor Exercise: Your Memory Support Plan

Use this plan if you are in trauma therapy or preparing for it.

- My signs that I am within my window:
- My signs I am flooding:
- My signs I am shutting down:
- My grounding tools before sessions:
- My grounding tools after sessions:
- Who I will contact if I feel unsafe:
- Routine that helps me return to life after sessions:
- A step-up plan if symptoms increase for more than two weeks.

Anchor Plan: Support Memory Work This Week

1) Practice the Then vs. Now skill once this week when an intrusion appears.
2) Do one grounding practice before and after any therapy session (or any difficult conversation).
3) Choose one life approach step after a heavy day (small, safe, real).
4) Share your Memory Support Plan with your therapist or one trusted support person.

Anchor Check

- I understand that trauma processing is structured, paced work.
- I can name at least two guardrails that keep memory work safe.
- I practiced the Then vs. Now skill at least once.
- I created a Memory Support Plan.
- I used grounding and connection to return to the present after a surge.

Closing reminder: Memories can be loud without being dangerous. The goal is not to erase the past. The goal is to stop living in it. With the right support and pacing, the brain can learn: "It is over."

Chapter 9
Boundaries: Protecting Healing Without Closing Your Heart

Anchor 9 — Boundaries
I can protect my healing and keep my heart open.

This anchor protects against reenactment patterns, resentment, burnout, and the belief that you must sacrifice yourself to be safe or loved. Trauma often teaches people to tolerate too much or to trust no one. Boundaries are the middle path: selective openness with clear limits.

Trauma can reshape relationships. PTSD can make you guarded, irritable, withdrawn, hyper-alert to tone, or terrified of disappointing people. Some survivors become isolated because closeness feels unsafe. Others over-function, people-please, or say yes when they mean no because conflict feels dangerous. Many people swing between the two: shutting down, then overextending, then shutting down again.

Boundaries are one of the most loving tools in trauma recovery. A boundary is not a wall. It is a clear line that protects safety, dignity, and healing. Boundaries help you stay connected without being consumed. They reduce the chance that relationships become another place where trauma repeats itself.

This chapter builds on Connection (Chapter 2) and Safety (Chapter 4), because boundaries work best when you have support and steadiness. When you have clear boundaries, your nervous system can relax. When boundaries are missing, your body may stay in threat mode—even around people you love.

What Boundaries Are (and What They Aren't).

Boundaries are about what you will do and what you will not do. They are not about controlling other people. A boundary is not "You must never raise your voice." A boundary is "If voices rise, I will pause the conversation and return later."

Boundaries are not punishments. They are protections. They create conditions where trust can grow.

Boundaries also do not require anger. You can set a boundary with warmth, calm, and clarity.

Why Trauma Makes Boundaries Hard

Many trauma survivors learned that boundaries were unsafe. Saying no may have led to punishment. Speaking up may have led to ridicule. Leaving may not have been possible. Some people learned that their needs did not matter, or that keeping peace was the only way to survive.

PTSD can also create boundary confusion in the other direction. Hypervigilance can make harmless comments feel threatening. Avoidance can make every request feel too big. The goal is not rigid boundaries. The goal is wise boundaries: clear enough to protect you, flexible enough to allow connection.

Three Boundary Foundations

1) Safety: Boundaries protect your nervous system's stability.
2) Dignity: Boundaries protect your worth and voice.
3) Recovery: Boundaries protect your treatment and practice time.

Before you set a boundary, ask: Which foundation is this protecting right now?

Boundaries With Yourself First

Some of the most important boundaries are internal. PTSD can push you into overexposure (too much trauma talk, too much doom-scrolling) or underexposure (avoid all feelings, avoid all people). Internal boundaries help you pace your own life.

Examples of internal boundaries:
- "I will not read triggering news before bed."
- "I will not have trauma conversations when I am already dysregulated."
- "I will practice grounding before I respond."

• "I will take a break instead of forcing through shutdown."

Internal boundaries are a way of caring for your nervous system—not a way of controlling it.

Relational Boundaries: Who, What, When, How

Relational boundaries become clearer when you specify four things:
• Who: with whom do I need a boundary?
• What: what behavior or pattern needs a limit?
• When: what is the signal that I need to act?
• How: what will I do when the boundary is crossed?

Boundaries are easier when they are specific. "Respect me" is vague. "Don't show up unannounced" is clear.

Boundary Scripts (Warm and Firm).

Use short sentences. Over-explaining can turn into anxiety. You do not need a courtroom case to set a limit.

Scripts you can use:
• "I want to talk about this, and I need us to keep our voices calm. If it escalates, I'll take a break and we can return later."
• "I'm not able to discuss this right now. I can talk tomorrow at 3:00."
• "I'm working on my PTSD recovery, and I'm limiting triggering content. Please don't send me

graphic videos or articles."
• "I care about you, and I'm not able to take this on. I can help in this smaller way: ______."
• "I'm not comfortable with that. Please stop."

Scripts for trauma disclosure boundaries:
• "I'm not ready to share details. Thank you for understanding."
• "I can tell you how I'm doing without telling the story."
• "I'm focusing on healing; I'm not discussing the trauma outside therapy right now."

Scripts for reassurance loops (when PTSD fuels repeated checking of safety or relationship tone):
• "I hear that you're scared. I'm here with you, but I won't answer that question again. Let's ground and take the next step."
• "I can offer presence, not certainty. Let's sit together for ten minutes."

Boundaries and Triggers in Close Relationships

Partners, family, and friends may not understand trauma triggers. They may say, "Just let it go," or "It was a long time ago." Sometimes they mean well and don't know what to do. Other times they are unsafe.

A helpful approach is to separate intent from impact. You can acknowledge intent while still setting a boundary about impact.

Example: “I know you’re trying to help. When you tell me to ‘get over it,’ my nervous system hears dismissal. What helps is: ‘I’m here. Do you want grounding or space?’”

Boundaries Around Conflict

Conflict can feel like danger in PTSD. Some people avoid it entirely. Others escalate quickly because the body is already activated. Boundaries create a plan for conflict that protects safety.

Two conflict boundaries:
• Time boundary: “We will talk for 15 minutes, then pause.”
• Tone boundary: “If voices rise or insults appear, we stop and return when calm.”

If conflict becomes emotionally abusive, threatening, or violent, seek professional help and safety planning. Healing cannot happen inside ongoing harm.

Boundaries as Exposure (Gently).

For many trauma survivors, setting a boundary is an exposure. It may trigger fear of rejection, anger, or abandonment. This is normal. You are training your nervous system that you can have needs and still be safe enough.

Start with small boundaries in safer relationships. Practice the script once. Notice your body. Ground afterward. Then return to life. This is how new learning happens.

Anchor Exercise: Your Boundary Plan (One Page).

Choose one relationship or one pattern to focus on this month.

- The boundary I need (one sentence):
- What it protects (safety, dignity, recovery):
- My warm-and-firm script:
- The action I will take if it's crossed:
- The support I need (who can help me follow through):
- What I will do to ground afterward:

Anchor Plan: One Boundary Practice This Week

1) Choose one boundary you have been avoiding.
2) Write the script in one or two sentences.
3) Practice saying it out loud once.
4) Use it in real life one time.
5) Ground afterward and record what you learned.

Anchor Check

- I can explain what a boundary is (what I will do / not do).
- I identified one boundary that protects my healing.
- I wrote a warm-and-firm script.
- I practiced one boundary in real life.
- I grounded afterward and recorded learning.

Closing reminder: Boundaries are not rejection. They are care. They protect your recovery and your relationships—so you can stay connected without losing yourself.

Chapter 10
Repair - Rebuilding Trust With Others—and With Yourself

Anchor 10 — Repair
Rupture isn't the end. Repair is a skill.

This anchor protects against hopelessness after conflict, shame-based withdrawal, and the belief that relationships are permanently damaged. Trauma often trains permanence: "It's ruined forever." Repair trains recovery: "We can return."

PTSD does not only affect symptoms. It affects patterns—how you show up, how you disappear, how you respond under stress, and how safe it feels to be close to other people. Trauma can lead to missed plans, irritability, emotional numbing, withdrawal, broken promises, or sudden intensity. Even when you are doing your best, the impact can create distance.

Repair is the skill that closes the gap between impact and intention. It is how relationships recover. It is also how you rebuild trust with yourself after PTSD has taken space. Many trauma survivors carry a quiet fear: "I ruin things." Repair teaches a different truth: "Rupture is not the end. Repair is a practice."

This chapter is not about forcing reconciliation with unsafe people. Repair is only appropriate when it is safe. If someone is abusive, threatening, or repeatedly violates boundaries, the work may be safety and distance—not repair. But in safe relationships, repair is a powerful part of healing.

Why PTSD Creates Rupture

PTSD can create rupture in several predictable ways:

- Hyperarousal: irritability, anger, sharp reactions, intolerance for noise or chaos.
- Avoidance: canceling, withdrawing, not responding, avoiding important conversations.
- Numbing: seeming distant, flat, disconnected, or uninterested.
- Threat scanning: misreading tone, facial expressions, or delays as danger.
- Shame: hiding struggles, lying by omission, pushing people away before they can reject you.

These patterns are not moral failure. They are survival adaptations. Repair is how you update those adaptations in safe relationships.

The Three Parts of Repair

Repair becomes easier when you keep it simple. Most repairs include three parts:

1) Acknowledge impact (without excuses).
2) Name the plan (what you're practicing / how you're getting support).
3) Invite collaboration (what helps and what boundaries protect healing).

You do not need perfect words. You need honesty and steadiness.

A Simple Repair Script (Use This Often).

Here is a short repair script you can use with a partner, friend, family member, coworker, or support person. Adjust the language to fit your voice:

- "I'm sorry for ______." (name the impact)
- "PTSD has been loud, and I'm working on it."
- "Here's what I'm practicing: ______." (one sentence)
- "Here's how you can help: ______." (one role)
- "Here's the boundary I'm using: ______." (to prevent repeating the pattern)
- "Thank you for staying with me."

Notice what the script does not include: a long defense. Trauma often makes people either over-explain or disappear. Repair is the middle path: brief truth + clear plan.

Repair With Yourself

Many trauma survivors are hard on themselves. When symptoms flare, self-talk becomes punishment: "I'm pathetic. I'm too much. I should be over this." Self-repair is the practice of returning to compassion and structure instead of condemnation.

Self-repair can look like:
- naming the moment: "I'm having a flare-up."
- normalizing: "This is a trauma response, not a failure."
- choosing one anchor: grounding, sleep, connection, or one approach step.
- asking for help early instead of waiting until you are overwhelmed.

Self-repair is not letting yourself off the hook. It is keeping yourself in the work without shame.

Repair After Avoidance: When You Cancel or Disappear

A common PTSD pattern is avoidance through withdrawal—canceling plans, leaving early, not returning calls, or going silent. People may interpret this as rejection. A repair helps prevent the story from growing.

Example repair:
• "I went quiet because I was overwhelmed. I care about you. I'm working on staying connected even when my symptoms spike."
• "I want to try again. Can we reschedule for a shorter time?"
• "If I start to shut down, I'll tell you and take a 10-minute reset instead of disappearing."

Short time-bound plans build trust more than big promises.

Repair After Irritability or Anger

Trauma can keep the body in fight energy. When the nervous system is already activated, small frustrations can feel like threats. If you snapped, raised your voice, or became harsh, a repair matters.

Example repair:
• "I raised my voice. That wasn't okay."
• "My body was activated, but I'm responsible for how I speak."
• "Next time I'm going to pause and take a break before I respond."
• "Thank you for giving me another chance."

Repair does not erase impact. It rebuilds safety by showing accountability.

When the Other Person Has Trauma Too

Sometimes both people carry trauma histories. That can create rapid escalation, shutdown, or mutual misunderstanding. If you notice repeated cycles, consider joint support: couples therapy, family therapy, or mediated conversations with a professional. The goal is not to assign blame. The goal is to build shared safety.

Repair Is Not Reconciliation

You can offer repair and still keep boundaries. You can acknowledge impact without returning to unsafe closeness. You can forgive without re-entering harm. In PTSD recovery, many people confuse repair with abandoning themselves. True repair includes self-protection.

Anchor Exercise: Your Repair Plan (One Page).

Use this page for one relationship that matters to you.

- The pattern PTSD creates (withdrawal, irritability, numbness, threat scanning):
- The impact on the relationship:
- My repair script (fill in the blanks):
- The boundary that prevents repetition:
- The support I need (therapist, accountability, practice plan):
- A small reconnection step (10–20 minutes):

Anchor Plan: One Repair This Week

1) Identify one relationship where PTSD has created distance.
2) Use the simple repair script once (brief, honest, no courtroom).
3) Name one plan you are practicing (grounding, sleep, approach, therapy task).
4) Take one small reconnection step (walk, coffee, text check-in).
5) Record what happened and what you learned.

Anchor Check

- I can explain the difference between rupture and repair.
- I used or drafted a simple repair script.
- I named one boundary that protects healing.
- I practiced one reconnection step.
- I practiced self-repair after a hard moment.

Closing reminder: PTSD can create distance, but distance is not destiny. Repair is how you come back—one honest step at a time.

Chapter 11
Meaning: Integrating Trauma Without Letting It Define You

Anchor 11 — Meaning
What happened matters—but it is not all that I am.

This anchor protects against identity foreclosure ("I am only a trauma survivor"), existential collapse, moral injury spirals, and hopelessness. Trauma can become a totalizing lens. Meaning helps you hold the trauma in truth without letting it become your entire identity. (Litz et al., 2009).

PTSD can shrink a life. It can make the world feel dangerous, the body feel unreliable, relationships feel complicated, and the future feel uncertain. Over time, many people begin to ask deeper questions: Who am I now? What does this mean? What do I do with what happened?

Meaning work is not about forcing a positive spin on trauma. It is not about pretending the trauma was "worth it." It is about integration—helping your life become bigger than what happened, even while honoring the pain. Meaning is how you move from survival to a life with direction.

This chapter comes after several stabilizing anchors for a reason. Meaning is easier to access when grounding and safety are stronger and when you have support. If you feel flooded or numb while reading, return to Grounding (Chapter 3) or Connection (Chapter 2). You can come back to meaning work slowly.

Meaning Is Not Bypassing

Some trauma survivors have been harmed by spiritual bypassing or forced positivity: "Everything happens for a reason," "Just forgive," "At least you're alive," or "Be grateful." These statements can feel like erasure. True meaning does not rush grief. It makes space for grief, anger, and loss.

A healthier definition: meaning is the way you relate to what happened. It is the story you choose to live now—not the trauma story alone.

Identity After Trauma: The 'Before and After' Split

Many people feel divided after trauma: the "before me" and the "after me." This split can create grief and confusion. You may miss who you were. You may feel ashamed of who you became under threat. You may feel disconnected from your own joy.

Integration does not mean going back to exactly who you were. It means letting the trauma become one chapter in a larger story. You can honor what changed without being consumed by it.

Grief: The Quiet Companion of PTSD

PTSD often includes grief. You may grieve safety, innocence, trust, time, relationships, health, or opportunities. You may grieve what you lost and what you never had. Some trauma survivors also grieve the person they were forced to become.

Grief does not mean you are failing. Grief is a sign that something mattered. Meaning work includes giving grief a place—without letting it become your whole home.

Moral Injury, Forgiveness, and Repair

For some people, the deepest pain is moral: a sense of having violated values, witnessed betrayal, or been unable to prevent harm. Moral injury can feel like contamination—"I am unforgivable."

Healing moral injury often involves truth, accountability where appropriate, grief, and repair where possible. It does not require self-punishment. It may involve forgiveness, but forgiveness cannot be forced. Forgiveness is not the same as reconciliation. Reconciliation requires safety and trust. Forgiveness (if chosen) is often a long process and may begin simply as: "I am willing to stop sentencing myself to endless punishment." (Litz et al., 2009).

If moral injury themes are strong, this is a place where professional therapy, trusted spiritual care, or both can be especially helpful. (Litz et al., 2009).

Values: A Compass When Feelings Are Loud

PTSD can make emotions feel like commands. Values are different. Values are chosen directions—how you want to live and who you want to be, even when emotions are intense.

Ask yourself:
• If fear were quieter, what would I move toward?
• What kind of person do I want to be in my relationships?
• What do I want to stand for, even in small ways?
• What would 'courage' look like this week?

Values do not remove pain. They give pain a direction to walk in.

Building a Life Bigger Than PTSD

Recovery is not only symptom reduction. It is life expansion. PTSD may always be part of your history, but it does not need to be the center of your days.

Choose two life domains to strengthen over the next month:

- Relationships: one weekly connection ritual.
- Health: one sleep or movement anchor.
- Growth: learning, education, skill-building.
- Work/service: one meaningful contribution.
- Creativity/play: a hobby without performance pressure.
- Faith/spirituality: a practice that grounds you.
- Rest: a protected recovery window.

Small actions in meaningful domains weaken PTSD's claim to be the main story.

Faith Lens (): Love, Lament, and the End of Condemnation

This book is for people from many faith traditions and those with none. This short section is offered for readers who carry spiritual struggle after trauma.

Many trauma survivors fear they are being punished, abandoned, or condemned. If faith is part of your life, it may help to remember this: trauma symptoms are not moral failure. Fear is not sin. Healing is not punishment.

In many faith traditions, lament is a legitimate spiritual language. Lament says: "This hurts. This was wrong. I need help." Lament does not pretend. It tells the truth in the presence of love.

If your faith community increases shame, pressure, or denial, it may not be a safe container for healing. A trauma-informed spiritual leader or counselor can help you separate love from accusation.

Anchor Skill: The Meaning Statement

A meaning statement is a single sentence that holds truth and direction. It is not a slogan. It is a compass.

Templates:
• "What happened was ________. It mattered. And now I am choosing ________."
• "I can carry grief and still move toward ________."
• "My trauma is part of my story, not my whole story. Today I will ________."

Keep the sentence simple enough to remember when you are tired.

Anchor Exercise: Your Meaning Map (One Page).

Write slowly. There are no perfect answers.

• What I lost (name one loss):
• What I still value (name one value):
• Who I want to be because of what I've learned (one trait):
• One relationship I want to strengthen:
• One action that expands my life this week:
• One sentence meaning statement:

Anchor Plan: One Meaning Practice This Week

1) Write one meaning statement and place it somewhere visible.
2) Choose one values-based action that has nothing to do with PTSD symptoms (a connection, hobby, contribution, faith practice, or rest).
3) Spend 10 minutes in gentle reflection or journaling once this week (stop if you flood; return to grounding).
4) If moral injury or spiritual struggle is intense, share it with a therapist or trusted support person instead of carrying it alone. (Litz et al., 2009).

Anchor Check

- I can explain the difference between meaning and bypassing.
- I named one loss and one value.
- I wrote one meaning statement.
- I took one values-based action this week.
- I used connection or grounding if meaning work felt heavy.

Closing reminder: Meaning is not a finish line. It is a direction. You are allowed to heal in layers, at your pace.

Chapter 12
Maintenance: Returning Is Success (Relapse Prevention and Stepping Up Support)

Anchor 12 — Maintenance
Return to your anchors after setbacks—maintenance is success.

This anchor protects against shame after setbacks, all-or-nothing thinking, abandoning practice when symptoms spike, and waiting too long to ask for help. PTSD is treatable, but it is also sensitive to stress, sleep disruption, life transitions, and cumulative strain. A maintenance plan keeps you steady when life gets loud.

PTSD recovery is not a straight line. Most people do not "graduate" and never have symptoms again. Instead, recovery looks like a series of returns—returning to grounding, returning to connection, returning to body basics, returning to approach, returning to truth. In PTSD, maintenance is not a backup plan. It is the plan.

This final anchor exists for two reasons. First, many people fear relapse after progress: "What if I lose what I gained?" Second, many people feel shame when symptoms flare: "I'm back at square one." Maintenance answers both fears with one steady truth: returning is success.

This chapter will help you recognize early warning signs, maintain the practices that keep your nervous system steady, and know when to step up support wisely. It will also help you build a life bigger than PTSD—because the strongest maintenance plan is not just symptom management. It is meaning, connection, and forward movement.

What 'Relapse' Often Looks Like in PTSD

In PTSD, relapse is often a quiet return of avoidance and safety behaviors—not always a dramatic breakdown. It can look like canceling plans again, isolating, scanning and checking more, using substances to numb, procrastinating, or shrinking your world.

Common early warning signs:
• Avoidance is increasing (you do less, leave earlier, stay closer to home).
• Hypervigilance is increasing (constant scanning, startle, irritability).
• Sleep is worsening and recovery after stress takes longer.
• You are withdrawing from safe relationships.
• Your trauma meanings get louder ("I'm not safe,"

"I'm broken," "I can't trust").
• You stop practicing anchors because you feel "too busy" or because things are "fine."

Notice: these are behavior shifts. PTSD stays strong when avoidance returns. Recovery stays strong when you return to approach and connection.

The Maintenance Triangle: Connection, Body, Approach

Most people stay well by maintaining three pillars. If one pillar weakens, the others matter even more.

1) Connection: you stay linked to support (therapist, support team, safe community).
2) Body basics: sleep, movement, nourishment, substance boundaries.
3) Approach: small ongoing steps that prevent avoidance from regrowing.

If all three weaken at the same time, symptoms often rise. Maintenance is noticing early and returning to one pillar immediately.

Setbacks Are Data, Not Verdicts

A setback can be triggered by illness, loss, conflict, transitions, anniversaries, or simply nervous system fatigue. The question is not "Why am I anxious again?" The question is: "What is my next right step?"

A compassionate reset script:
• Name it: "I'm having a flare-up."
• Normalize: "This is what PTSD does under stress."
• Choose one pillar today (connection, body, or approach).
• Take one small step (10–20% stretch).
• Ask for help early instead of waiting until you are overwhelmed.

The 24-Hour Rule: Don't Let Avoidance Steal Two Days

A practical maintenance rule: if you avoid something today, do one small approach step within 24 hours. This keeps avoidance from becoming a new habit.

Examples:
• If you canceled a plan, send a text and reschedule a shorter version.
• If you avoided driving, sit in the car for two minutes and ground.
• If you avoided a conversation, write one sentence and set a time to talk.
• If you avoided a place, drive near it and return home as planned.

This is not punishment. It is training. Avoidance grows fast. Approach must return quickly.

Schedule Maintenance Like a Prescription

The most common reason people lose ground is not loss of knowledge—it's loss of practice. The brain returns to what it rehearses.

Two scheduling options:
- Option A: Weekly anchor appointment (20–30 minutes). Put it on your calendar.
- Option B: Daily micro-anchor (5–10 minutes) tied to an existing habit (after coffee, after lunch, before bed).

If you wait to feel motivated, PTSD often wins. Schedule beats mood.

When to step up support (Again).

Stepping up is not failure. It is wisdom. Consider increasing professional support if:
- Avoidance or symptoms are worsening week to week.
- You have frequent dissociation or feel unsafe.
- Nightmares, panic, or intrusive memories feel unmanageable.
- You are relying on substances to cope most days.
- Sleep is severely disrupted for more than two weeks.
- You are not improving despite returning to practice.

If you have thoughts of harming yourself or feel you might act on suicidal thoughts, seek urgent help immediately. You deserve rapid support.

Anchor Skill: The Return Plan

Create a simple, repeatable plan for flare-ups. The plan should be short enough to use when you are stressed.

Return Plan:
1) Ground (3 minutes).
2) Connect (text/call one support person).
3) Body anchor (sleep cue, walk, nourishment).
4) One approach step (small, safe).
5) Record one sentence of learning: "Today I returned by ______."

Anchor Exercise: Your Maintenance Plan (One Page).

Fill this out now—before you need it. Share it with one support person if possible.

- My early warning signs (top 5):
- My top avoidance pattern:
- My top safety behaviors that creep back:
- My 3 maintenance practices (easy, repeatable):
- My body basics anchors (sleep/movement/substances):
- My connection plan (who/when/how):

• My professional plan (therapist/doctor; when to re-engage):
• My step-up plan (what I do if I'm not improving):
• My reminder to myself (one sentence):

Anchor Plan: Your Maintenance Week

1) Complete your one-page maintenance plan.
2) Schedule one weekly anchor appointment (20–30 minutes).
3) Choose one body anchor to practice on 4 days (sleep or movement counts).
4) Do one values-based action that expands your life (connection, contribution, creativity, rest).

Anchor Check

• I can name my early warning signs.
• I built a Return Plan for flare-ups.
• I created a one-page maintenance plan.
• I scheduled practice instead of waiting for motivation.
• I chose one values-based action this week.

Closing reminder: Returning is the work. Returning is the skill. Returning is success.

Appendix A
Anchors at a Glance

1. Connection — Needing support does not mean you are 'too broken.' It means your nervous system is responding to real threat learning—and support is one of the ways PTSD is treated.

2. Grounding — "This is a memory, not a current threat."

3. Safety — "Right now, in this moment, I am safe enough to take my next step."

4. Body — "My body learned danger. My body can learn recovery."

5. Story — "Trauma lies in meanings. I can learn to tell the truth."

6. Choice — "I have choices now, even small ones."

7. Approach — "Avoidance keeps trauma powerful. Approach gives me my life back."

8. Memory — "The trauma is over. My brain can learn that."

9. Boundaries — "I can protect my healing and keep my heart open."

10. Repair — "Rupture isn't the end. Repair is a skill."

11. Meaning — "What happened matters—but it is not all that I am."

12. Maintenance — "Return to your anchors after setbacks—maintenance is success."

Appendix B
References

American Psychiatric Association. (2022). Diagnostic and statistical manual of mental disorders (5th ed., text rev.). American Psychiatric Association Publishing.

Bisson, J. I., Berliner, L., Cloitre, M., Forbes, D., Jensen, T. K., Lewis, C., Monson, C. M., Olff, M., Pilling, S., Riggs, D. S., Roberts, N. P., & Shapiro, F. (2019). The International Society for Traumatic Stress Studies new guidelines for the prevention and treatment of PTSD: Methodology and development process. Journal of Traumatic Stress, 32(4), 475–483. https://doi.org/10.1002/jts.22421

Brewin, C. R., Andrews, B., & Valentine, J. D. (2000). Meta-analysis of risk factors for posttraumatic stress disorder in trauma-exposed adults. Journal of Consulting and Clinical Psychology, 68(5), 748–766. https://doi.org/10.1037/0022-006X.68.5.748

Department of Veterans Affairs & Department of Defense. (2023). VA/DoD clinical practice guideline for the management of posttraumatic stress disorder and acute stress disorder. https://www.healthquality.va.gov/guidelines/MH/ptsd/

Foa, E. B., Hembree, E. A., & Rothbaum, B. O. (2007). Prolonged exposure therapy for PTSD: Emotional processing of traumatic experiences: Therapist guide. Oxford University Press.

Litz, B. T., Stein, N., Delaney, E., Lebowitz, L., Nash, W. P., Silva, C., & Maguen, S. (2009). Moral injury and moral repair in war veterans: A preliminary model and intervention strategy. Clinical Psychology Review, 29(8), 695–706. https://doi.org/10.1016/j.cpr.2009.07.003

National Institute for Health and Care Excellence. (2018). Post-traumatic stress disorder (NICE guideline NG116). https://www.nice.org.uk/guidance/ng116

Ozer, E. J., Best, S. R., Lipsey, T. L., & Weiss, D. S. (2003). Predictors of posttraumatic stress disorder and symptoms in adults: A meta-analysis. Psychological Bulletin, 129(1), 52–73. https://doi.org/10.1037/0033-2909.129.1.52

Schnurr, P. P., Hamblen, J. L., Wolf, J., Coller, R., Collie, C., Fuller, M. A., Holtzheimer, P. E., Kelly, U., Lang, A. J., McGraw, K., Morganstein, J. C., Norman, S. B., Papke, K., Petrakis, I., Riggs, D., Sall, J. A., Shiner, B., Wiechers, I., & Kelber, M. S. (2024). The management of posttraumatic stress disorder and acute stress disorder: Synopsis of the 2023 U.S. Department of Veterans Affairs and U.S. Department of Defense clinical practice guideline. Annals of Internal Medicine, 177(3), 363–374. https://doi.org/10.7326/M23-2757

Shapiro, F. (2018). Eye movement desensitization and reprocessing (EMDR) therapy: Basic principles, protocols, and procedures (3rd ed.). The Guilford Press.

About the Author

Cindy H. Carr, D.Min., MACL, has spent her vocational life walking alongside people in the slow, often unseen work of formation and change. Her career has been intentionally bi-vocational, shaped by years of pastoring, business leadership, and pastoral counseling—always with a focus on helping people live with greater clarity, dignity, and wholeness.

She earned a Master of Arts in Church Leadership from Eastern Mennonite Seminary and completed her doctoral work at Liberty University. Over the years, she served multiple churches in Virginia's Shenandoah Valley in a variety of pastoral and leadership capacities.

In this season of life, Cindy's work has shifted from direct leadership into writing and education. Through her books, she helps readers implement formation-based principles she has taught throughout her career—practices centered on identity, connection, return, and steady growth without shame.

Learn more about Cindy and her work at

CindyHCarr.com

www.ingramcontent.com/pod-product-compliance
Lightning Source LLC
LaVergne TN
LVHW011031110826
845149LV00015B/3379
* 9 7 8 1 9 7 1 1 9 2 3 2 1 *